## QUEEN OF THE MIST

*MRS. ANNA ("ANNIE") TAYLOR*

Shot Horseshoe Falls (165 feet) October 24, 1901, and survived—a feat never before attempted.

Entered barrel one and one-half miles above the Falls.

Was in barrel one hour and fifteen minutes. Had 32 pounds of air in barrel; 100 pounds weight on foot of barrel. Rescued six hundred yards below Falls, on Canadian shore.

# QUEEN

## *OF THE*

# *MIST*

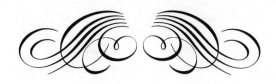

## JOAN MURRAY

BEACON PRESS
BOSTON

BEACON PRESS
25 Beacon Street
Boston, Massachusetts 02108-2892
www.beacon.org

BEACON PRESS BOOKS
are published under the auspices of
the Unitarian Universalist Association of Congregations.

Frontispiece photo by Samuel M. Golden.
Used by permission of the Local History Department,
Niagara Falls, New York, Public Library

04 03 02 01 00 99   8 7 6 5 4 3 2

This book is printed on recycled acid-free paper that contains at least 20
percent postconsumer waste and meets the uncoated paper ANSI/NISO
specifications for permanence as revised in 1992.

Text design by Anne Chalmers
Composition by Wilsted & Taylor Publishing Services

LIBRARY OF CONGRESS CATALOGING-IN-PUBLICATION DATA

Murray, Joan.
Queen of the mist / Joan Murray.
p.   cm.
ISBN 0-8070-6852-7 (alk. paper)
1. Taylor, Annie Edson, 1838–1921—Poetry.
2. Women stunt performers—Niagara Falls (N.Y. and Ont.)—Poetry.
3. Daredevils—Niagara Falls (N.Y. and Ont.)—Poetry.
4. Niagara Falls (N.Y. and Ont.)—History—Poetry.   I. Title.
PS3563.U7694Q44   1999
811'.54—dc21        98-42932

FOR JIM

who, with kindness and grace,

has welcomed Annie into our lives

# Contents

# I

# THE CALL

Sealed in my barrel,
with an anvil clamped beneath my feet,
I sailed upright,
listened for Holleran's tap—
twice on the lid staves
—then they cut me loose.
I rode low, scraped the bottom stones,
clipped a rock, caught the current.
In a moment I was at the brink,
thudding on the cusp—
pitching forward, breathless, blind—
from a womb
of my own making.

*Niagara!—over* me!—*under* me!—
I spilled into it from every pore,
lost myself
in the blackness of its roar.
Something opened—grew wide—tore—
till every part of me was new:
Brain. Eyes. Tongue
—down to the wet soles in my shoes.
I took my measure, checked my sex
and, pleased with what I'd made,
I slapped my back between the blades
and took a breath
of consciousness.

What did they expect to find when they got at me?
At first, the lid was stuck, my air was thin,
I was at their mercy.

And then it was a hacksaw that revealed me:
Up from the river I came—
I was wet—and dizzy
—and deafened by the ringing of the bells,
but I could tell
that every part of me
was *new!*

I was exactly what I had expected:
I was *alive*—
and *I* was what I had to show for it.
So I didn't stand serenely
like Jesus in the Jordan on his baptism day,
the sky opening and closing around him—
I had to work my *own* riggings,
supply my *own* light
—on that day I finally
came *alive*—

there—beneath the mantel of the Horseshoe,
with the slender Bridal Veil, shimmering to my right
—and everyone's eyes on me,
everyone's hands, handing me along,
steadying me—reaching out to touch me.
You can see the *Hallelujah* in their eyes—
for that one moment—
before their lids screwed down again,
and they realized
I wasn't quite what they'd expected.

[ THE PHENOMENON ]
The church bells rang on both sides of the river,
spreading rumors of "a miracle."

And from everywhere they came to have a glimpse of it
—scrambling down the gorge
as if it were the final call at the final resurrection,
and then they saw me—
a puzzling phenomenon:
a woman, short and plain—and only slightly bruised,
moving dizzily among them
like a fly hatched by mistake in the winter sun.
I saw their puzzled looks—
and wondered if they'd like to put me back!

I had done what all the scientists had said no one could do
—I was, in fact, the first to ever try.
And though I lied about my age, I was really sixty-three,
I was plump and nearly grey
when they poured into the gorge to look at me—
a baffling phenomenon:
I was not a beauty or a man, yet there I was,
the center of attention.
Someone asked about my college degree,
they started questioning my intentions.
Then my manager came forward and gave a little wave
and handed me a single red carnation.

Now they waited for me to regale them:
they asked for details, observations—
*"gory* details!" someone called (he must have seen
my drooping shoulder and my head bruise),
but I was still too stunned to speak—
I was a difficult phenomenon.
Yet I tried to find some words that would please them.
But how could I *begin* to explain
what had occurred in that barrel

—that had changed my life into my *own* possession?
So I looked into their eyes, I even found a smile,
and I told them, *I am alive.*

[ DOING CARTWHEELS ]

I know you're wondering how I thought of such a thing—
an educated woman, at the beginning of the twentieth century,
and if I had a Muse to illuminate my story,
you might see the hand of Fate—
but all I can tell you on my own
is that my plan *was born of Necessity.*
I was in Bay City, Michigan,
a lumber town on the Saginaw
—in a studio with gaslights
and a bargain-priced, hardwood floor.
And since it was a time of promise and prosperity,
I found credit for a secondhand piano.

I had a hundred students from the finest families
and taught ballroom dance and manners, fall through spring
—culminating in a coming-out cotillion
into lumber-town "society."
But then the number dropped to seventy.
They were strained by the expense
of year-round classes,
their requisite corsages and livery coaches,
and embroidered satin gowns,
shipped C.O.D. from Chicago and New York.
So I modified my theme to "rhythmic dance"—
they got by in local taffeta for their seasonal recitals.

And when enrollment fell to fifty,
I gave them "Summer Promenades" and "Winter's Eve Tableaux"—

where they could learn some simple movements in a week—
and stroll about the streets
—or pose as the Fates or Muses (in homemade crepe paper gowns).
When the count had dropped to thirty,
I switched to acrobatics. (I had studied physical culture
and was a certified instructor
—the girls were quite amazed to see my cartwheels).
But my rent was overdue, I'd run up a tab for food,
I needed winter boots,
and enrollment fell to twenty.

I held an evening tea-and-social for the parents.
I showed them my diploma from the Normal School in Albany.
I told them where I'd taught and been a principal.
Why, I could tutor *every academic subject*
—teach them French or Spanish—or instrumental music.
Why, I could *even* teach their daughters *proper English*
—Couldn't they see them,
with improved elocution,
moving comfortably "in fashionable society"?
But when I asked them what they wanted
—how I could *serve* them or their children,
someone asked *if I'd demonstrate my cartwheels.*

[ A WOMAN'S OPTIONS ]

I walked in my despair along the Saginaw—
listening to the water toss itself against the darkness,
watching it rush headlong on the same purposeless course
it had been following for seven thousand years.
Now and then, a human thing—
a piece of fence, a box or barrel—
bobbed to the surface, was whirled and upended,
battered from bank to bank—and kept on going.

I watched it twist beneath the same bruised moon
that was inching through the same forsaken sky
it had inched through fifty million times
with its borrowed light and empty mythologies.

I could see it was the ending of a story—
where a deluded mortal wakens from a dream.
My teaching days were gone—along with Saginaw "society."
Even if I placed an advertisement,
or paid a boy to put my card in every door on every city street,
at last I understood: it was now the twentieth century,
and no one wanted waltzes, no one set a value on civility.
I saw the options left me—
the options of all single, destitute women over forty:
I could turn to poorhouse charity
or keep my self-sufficiency by scrubbing pots and privies
—and spend my nights doing other people's laundry.

But another option spread itself before me:
I looked down at the river—the current that could *not* refuse me
—and its lethal invitation held the *one endurable* future I could see.
I could see where it would drag me:
Up to Saginaw Bay and down through Lake Huron.
Down the St. Clair, the Detroit, and into Lake Erie.
Two hundred miles more till I reached the Niagara—
and there I saw what I'd become:
a splinter of wreckage, a shard of myself,
a thing beyond caring or meaning.
—And I wanted to *be* that—
I climbed the rail, stretched my arms—and *gave* myself to it.

How can I explain how something lifted me then—
not only off the railing and up from the river—

but held me hovering above a chasm more luminous than heaven.
And when it set me down again,
soaked to my skin, with my hair dripping down my neck,
I knew I'd seen—Niagara Falls.
*Niagara!*
I had seen it once before
from my father's wagon, the autumn I turned seven.
I remember how I dropped my apple from my hand
as my eyes climbed its brilliant plume of mist,
rising effortlessly to the light—

And how the rim of the Horseshoe came in sight,
and from its roiling crucible, the sound—
—the *sound!*—as a billion simultaneous poundings
struck like thunder every knot down my spine.
I had no words then to describe its impact,
no means to distinguish its energy from mine.
It imparted everything to me
(a farmer's daughter from Auburn!)
—It entered me—vision and concussion,
and coded itself in my nerves and my brain.
And now in Bay City, on a rail above the Saginaw,
it revived itself: *A ledge* where I could leap—to *save* my life.

[ A LONG PREPARATION ]

At once I knew the summons in that rescue:
Since the days of P. T. Barnum
half a century before,
all America knew "the challenge of Niagara."
It seemed every other year
another challenger appeared.
If he were a scientist,
there'd be reports in *Leslie's Weekly*

with pictures of his patented invention:
a cocoon-like boat or inflated suit—
an enormous rubberized gyroscope
—or other useless whirligig contraption.

And if he were an athlete,
there'd be columns on his regimen and stamina—
his chin-ups and his push-ups—
how he'd earned his toughness
in a Channel swim
—or at the fists of John L. Sullivan.
But despite their boasts and ballyhoo,
the clamoring of the press,
and Barnum's old prediction
of "eternal fame and wealth,"
in the end, not one of them
had the nerve to see it through.

So Niagara was still waiting,
unchallenged and unclaimed,
and what had I to lose to take it?
Hadn't I just stepped across a brink—
where something's hand shot through the mist
—to pluck me by the neck
and set me down?
And whether it came from the farthest stars
(or maybe from some corner of my brain),
it led me home to my boarding house,
and when I opened the front door,
I already knew its plan.

[ FIAT! ]

Then—like the Virgin Mary—
I was quickened:

*10*

I got down on my knees
and spread two lengths of pattern stock
and began to sketch a shape:
I rounded it and tapered it,
added and erased
—till I knew it would accommodate my size.
In the morning, I bought some cardboard sheets.
And, cutting them, with a care I usually saved for silk,
I had my second skin
of cardboard barrel staves.
I laced them piece to piece with twine
—then crawled inside the thing.

After, I sent a boy to fetch the cooper.
I seated him in the parlor with a cup of tea.
I didn't look up as I talked,
but stared at the gold rim of my cup—
my hand trembling
—not from fear—
but from the excitement of hearing my plan materialize.
When he finally understood,
he stormed through the door (with a trail of oaths
and all my neighbors' eyes).
But three days later,
once I'd pawned my mother's Milanese lace cloth,
I called him back
and watched him change his mind.

And then I got to supervise his workers:
I picked each piece of thick Kentucky oak.
I held it to the light,
examined it—for warps, knots, insect bores
—the slightest sign

of any imperfection.
I oversaw the oiling and the joining,
the welding of the hasp and iron bands.
I satisfied myself
with the articulation of the hatch.
I ignored their laughter.
I admired the lines of my vessel
—the contours (resembling mine)
—of the thing they said would be my tomb.


[ NIGHT TRAIN ]

I left Bay City, just as dark was coming,
and under the thickening stars,
I counted out each second of that night:
metal on metal—pounding an endless two-note meter
that took me down the peninsula,
across the basin and on to Niagara.
*Pounding, Pounding,*
so I couldn't sleep.
All night I watched the dark
—now and then a spark leapt from the track
and flickered for a second
in the grass.


And then it was miles and miles of blackness
—then a depot with a glove factory
—then a rail spur with a shoe factory.
*Pounding, Pounding,*
past a granery. Past a sawmill and a foundry.
Finally stopping at a station where a hackman's horse
drooped its head beneath a gaslight
—and the hackman,

calling up and down for passengers,
saw nothing spilling out
but barrels.

*Pounding, Pounding,*
past the mazy blur of forests—
past a bent shape
lit by a campfire—
past a shack—invisible—except for its single window—
which floated on the center of the night
—a framed and disembodied light—
wandering the firmament,
uncertain where to land
and finally dropping out of sight
behind me.

*Pounding, Pounding,*
past the small stations—
with their slurred goodbyes,
the handshakes missed, the kisses that didn't land right.
Everything hurrying because the train was leaving
—so that even the urgent reminder
or the long-rehearsed blessing
came too late from below the window—
lips moving, but nothing heard,
and the train pulling off
in its hiss of steam.

*Pounding, Pounding,*
till the light gathered,
and there, at last, was Niagara
—arranged along its gorge—with all its grand hotels!
It was Sunday—I heard the pealing bells,

and envisioned, through the mist,
that a thousand white-gowned sleepers
were rising from their beds,
and hurrying to their windows
to salute me
as I came.

Then the pounding stopped, and the station came in sight—
with my manager, Tussie Russell
(and his bunch of red carnations).
I had met him once in Saginaw,
and now as I descended from the train,
I saw him wave to a woman
coming from the forward car.
I called his name—he recovered quickly,
and gave me his bouquet
—and told me he had booked me
in a boarding house.

# II

# THE GATE

We came by hack (over rutted streets—
past rows of shacks—and drab, worker houses).
I had hoped to see the Falls
—not as a condemned man
watches the gallows rising in the yard
to prepare himself for the role he has to play
—but eager as a bride, straining through the crowd
for the first glimpse of her spouse
at the altar on their wedding day.
But Russell waved my hopes away,
complained that I was late,
and shouted to the driver
to hurry to the boarding house.

I was barely in the door
when a crowd of reporters
swarmed from the parlor,
calling out questions, scribbling descriptions,
till I asked them, "Please,
out of decency, let me have a moment to myself."
Then George Billings, who ran the house,
took me up to my room
and welcomed me warmly,
but nervously,
by pointing out the furnishings
—(he *even* lifted the edge of the spread
to show me the chamber pot!).

I thanked him for his "thorough hospitality,"
then turned to comb my hair.
But footsteps came storming up the stairs,

and Russell, opening my door,
said I was acting like a "stuck-up prima donna."
Did I know the trouble
of assembling a corps
of *"international* reporters?"
(He must have *known*
that someone had popped over from Toronto.)
But I bit my tongue,
replaced my hat
and started down.

As I entered, I noticed their paper-thin smiles,
their pencils fidgeting to get at me—
and poke me with their question:
"So you're doing it *for money?*"
"Just how do you intend to *make a killing?*"
one of them quipped
as Dolly Billings brought in some sandwiches.
I stood up then and begged to be excused,
explaining, I'd been traveling all night,
and hadn't really slept
and wasn't used to getting such attention
—"And, for now, my *one* intention
is *to be alive.*"

[ A TOAST ]

"Mrs. Taylor will sit here tonight,"
George Billings told a man in a frock coat
(who, rising from his chair, applauded the idea
though it was clear
he didn't like the new arrangement).
Billings had the table's head, I had the foot,

and Dolly took the spot nearest the kitchen.
Russell was on my left, next to Caroline his wife.
The man, whose "place" I occupied,
was seated on my right.
When Billings introduced the group,
he called him "the professor."

"Did you know, Mrs. Taylor," the professor asked,
"that the story of the Falls begins with a woman?
Not exactly like yourself,
she was a beautiful young maiden,
sent by her tribe as a sacrifice
to their Thunder God who lived below the Falls.
Her story is hopelessly confused—
they say she paddled naked in an oarless canoe,
but whatever ill her people had been suffering—
some plague or famine—ended at once,
and she's been known ever since
as the 'Maid of the Mist.' "

Then Billings raised his glass:
"To Mrs. Taylor—not the *Maid*—but the *Queen*
of the Mist!" and as each guest took a sip, he laughed—
"Niagara's quite the place for the ladies!
Even Miss Sarah Bernhardt visited our Falls
one winter long ago. She gave me a five-dollar bill
—more than my father made all week—
to take her sledding down the ice bridge in the gorge.
I tell you, I'd know what to do today
if Sarah Bernhardt wrapped her pretty legs around me!"
(Though Dolly scolded him,
she was laughing like the rest of us.)

Then the professor raised his glass in my direction:
"Be careful, Mrs. Taylor.
Tonight we may joke, but Niagara isn't kind—
it's taken many lives—mostly accidents and suicides—
but a few like you, who've come to put its patience to the test:
Maud Willard was another, a beautiful young actress—
she merely tried to ride some rapids
half a mile below the Falls
—but they pulled her out this spring."
"Now stop this!" Billings said
(he was red in the face).
"*No one* needs to hear about Maud Willard."

[ MAUD WILLARD ]

She had been beautiful they said.
But that night—when I *saw* her—she was swollen and bruised,
and stank from what she'd been through in her barrel.
I held my handkerchief to my nose as she began to speak.
I thought she'd come to warn me—
though she never spoke of me
(it was one long soliloquy!)
—and I remembered—they had said she'd been an actress.
That night she took my bedroom for a stage,
and, like it or not, I was her audience.
When my eyes became accustomed to what little light there was,
I saw her lips were blue. She winced each time she moved
—maybe to prove she was suffering.

She said she hadn't even *thought* about *the Falls:*
"A plunge from the Falls had *never* been done
—Perhaps never will be," she said (with no hint of irony—
no reference to me or my intentions).

20

She had chosen the Lower Rapids—
it was a simple, familiar run:
shoot some rapids, skirt a whirlpool—then bob to the Canadian side.
It already had been done (at least a dozen times).
I wondered why, then, would she even *want* to try—
though I didn't ask her—Instead I asked her to sit down.
But she waved away my offer
and paced around my room,
covering all the space as she had probably learned on stage.

She said she shot the rapids quickly.
As far as she could tell, she wasn't even scratched
—and assuming the worst was over, she began to relax,
and when the roar had almost quelled, she wet her lips,
and fluffed her hair, and arranged the bow tie of her middy blouse.
Then she started practicing her smile, knowing all the while,
that an Edison camera, mounted on a flat car,
was rolling beside her in the gorge.
She'd brought her little dog and stroked it occasionally.
She planned to step out daintily—
and hold the puppy to her cheek
—assuming the pose she had calculated
would maximize her publicity.

She was not the sort of woman
to be concerned—with less pleasant possibilities.
Her looks had always made things easy.
In thirty seconds, she'd be a celebrity.
In sixty, a dime museum queen.
She understood timing. She had her speech rehearsed
—though she'd tucked a copy in the pocket of her skirt
(just in case she stumbled on her lines).

And then she felt the dog's heart quicken,
and for the briefest moment, she could not imagine why.
But then a sickening feeling swept over her
for she knew the whirlpool had her
—and she hadn't planned for this contingency.

She couldn't know, of course,
how long it would hold her in its embrace,
tossing her limbs as it led her through the motions of its dance.
The air inside grew thin. The puppy yelped.
And though it was useless to call for help,
she called for more than an hour—but no one heard her call.
Six hours later, they snagged her barrel with a hook
—and someone dragged her in.
When they ripped off the lid,
the dog was standing on her head. It skittered out and ran.
But when she didn't move, someone reached inside
and grabbed her hair—jerking her face to the torch light
—and they could tell that she was dead.

By then it was too dark to hoist her up the gorge,
so they left her lying on the bank, where a crowd of workmen
clambered down and spent the night beside her—
singing crude songs and drinking
—till it was light enough—to drag her by her ankles up the slope.
She turned away as she told me that
—and suddenly I saw—I was alone.
Why had she come to me?—like a bruised wife,
wailing to her husband's mistress but leaving him unaccused.
I had no way to compensate her for her tragedy
—even by my failure (if that is what she wanted).
And I didn't need Maud Willard to paint her grisly picture
—I had dreamed more gruesome endings on my own.

What had I been dreaming—
when a log fell suddenly through the grate,
exploded in the embers and woke me?
It wasn't fire I saw then—
but tongues of water, breaking over wood,
probing for an opening—trying to drag it down.
*Was it a warning?*
At dawn, my barrel would be launched in a trial run
(I hadn't seen it since I'd handed it to Russell
at a depot, back in Michigan).
Now I pictured it on the brink
and was filled with numbing dread
—a thing I couldn't lavish on myself.
So I dressed with fumbling hands and ran into the night—
I had to find my barrel—and touch it one more time
before the morning.

I listened for the murmur of the Falls
and followed its direction down to Falls Street
—and turning the corner, caught a chilly blast of mist—
that pursued me past the Lyceum Theater
and the International Hotel
(both quiet at that time of night),
but the street lamps, with their strange electric lights,
showed a woman, darting through the darkened windows.
At first, I didn't realize who she was
—I didn't know I'd put my best hat on—
the one with the ostrich plume
(you may have seen it in the photo
where I'm standing with my barrel
and a cat curled on the rim
—the cat who drowned that morning
in the trial run).

From the moment that Russell
had told me of that test, I had argued against it.
But Truesdale, the riverman, insisted.
He had done some sort of trial
for each fool who'd shot the rapids
and each boaster "who had come to try the Falls"
(they always sent a cat ahead,
and when it drowned,
they packed up their ambitions and went home).
Truesdale believed that "such concern for safety"
would protect him from arrest
if things went badly.
And Russell was ready with his lies:
—whatever happened to the cat,
he would tell the press,
"Yes, it had nine lives!"


At the end of Falls Street,
I approached the lighted portico of the State Park Hotel,
and, ascending its steps, saw fastened to its door,
a placard that proclaimed (in three-inch type):
"Mrs. Taylor's Fateful Barrel
Is On Display Inside."
Russell had arranged it with the manager
(for a fee I *never* saw)
as a way to lure the tourists in.
That night, the manager was gone,
and the bellhop was asleep behind the desk.
He had a hooked rug draped across his lap
(a cat had crawled there for a nap
and would likely stay till morning).
I studied the serene face of the boy,
the cat opened one eye.

I decided not to wake them,
but tiptoed by
till I found my barrel in a cavernous lobby
with mahogany pillars and ensconced electric lights.
I ran my hand along its sides
and saw where "Queen of the Mist"
had been scrawled in white between the iron bands.
Russell must have come that night
and painted Billings' line—
a line I never liked:
I never wanted to be *"Queen"* of anything
—and *"Mist"* was hardly a kingdom!
But I knocked the lid for luck.
The boy stirred, and the cat purred as I passed.
I blessed them both
and quietly shut the door.

[ "ONE OF MINE" ]

I walked back slowly past the grand hotels
to the other end of Falls Street.
And there, the street lights died,
and the side streets narrowed
to cobblestone lanes with rooming houses,
and cottages where workmen slept,
two to a bed, or beside their wives and children.

From a darkened doorway,
a woman staggered toward me.
I smelled the brandy on her breath.
She was pale but pretty in a summer dress
and an elaborate silk shawl
—hemmed with a foot of gilded fringe
(the kind of thing the gentry used to drape pianos).

"Here, dear. Have one of mine," she said,
opening her purse and trying to press
a silver dollar in my hand.
Her eyes were swimming in her head.
"Tonight I did some waltzing with the gentlemen.
And from the look of you,
I'll bet you didn't do the same."

I pushed her hand away,
and coins spilled to the stones
and rolled among the last October leaves.
She stared at the ground. And then at me.
"Don't touch my money," she warned—
"Go get some on your back—You must know
some tricks with your fancy hat!—What's your specialty?"

A block away, I could still make out her shape—
kneeling among the leaves,
and still hear her calling out a breathless slur of insults:
"Don't think you can fool me
with your high and mighty act.
I know who you are—
You're a whore—just like me."

[ PRODIGALS ]

"So here you are—I was sure you'd bolted."
It was Russell on the outside steps—
not even light—and Caroline, his wife,
up and dressed, reaching her arms out to embrace me,
rubbing my back so motherly
(and she not half my age),
showing how afraid she must have been
—not for my sake—But that I might have slipped away.

"If something had happened," she said,
and though she stopped at that,
I understood her meaning:
I was Russell's *one big chance* for money.

Before he'd met me,
he was a small-time promoter of platform divers
—boys he'd plucked naked off the rotting lumber,
stacked along Saginaw Bay.
He had them dressed in bright, striped swimsuits
that buttoned to their throats,
and he'd designed a vast array of jerryrigged machinery,
which he rolled from town to town like Caesar's army:
There was a diving tank and a fifty-foot tower,
a crimson carpet and a gilded ladder,
a parapet with a crown of lights
—and all those wild boys in stripes!

On the day I went to interview him,
the boys were chuckling at the bottom of the ladder
"Want to give it a try, Miss?" the tallest one asked.
I could see that each of them
(even the smallest freckled one)
had been briefed on all the details of my plan
—though Russell had agreed to my demand for *secrecy*.
But now, months later, I had the unintended pleasure
of frightening him that night
—like a diver in the middle of a dive,
who's just spied
an *empty* tank!

And what an *added* pleasure
—to picture him—hungover yet alarmed

when he found me gone.
I knew he'd been out late with the reporters.
At ten, he brought the whole corps to the parlor
to show off his dainty wife.
Then off they went again
(with Russell charging each round to my name!).
He probably dragged the last few tipsy ones
all the way to the State Park Hotel—
so they could stand applauding while he took a can of paint—
and scribbled "Queen of the Mist" across my barrel staves.

And now, though he hadn't shaved,
he was up and dressed—and rubbing his eyes—
which looked redder than the coals in Dolly Billings' stove,
where slabs of thick-sliced bacon were sizzling in a pan,
and the guests were pouring in for breakfast—
as if a celebration were in progress—
as if I'd just been saved (from some perilous change of plans).
I had coffee, eggs, and bacon,
and as I mopped my yolk with bread,
I glanced into the kitchen—
where Russell sat, holding his head
—without an appetite for anything.


[ THE MOB ]

Voices in the street?—A mob moving!
Hoots and shouts I couldn't make out yet,
and with my one window on the alley,
I couldn't see *who* was coming
—but they were coming for *me*
—and I knew they meant to do me harm.
I'd had threats from cranks and crazies,

condemnations by church ladies,
and warnings from the Niagara Falls police.
When word had gotten out that the cat had died,
the humane society led an outcry
—till someone nailed a dead cat to the door.
To appease the mayor's wife (who had "a delicate nature"),
Chief Dinan gave a statement to the press
that he was planning to arrest me.
And at dinner that night, I heard the kitchen bell
and Constable Eagan (who patrolled that beat)
told Dolly he'd be watching in the morning,
and if I meant to try my stunt—
I'd be charged with *attempted suicide*
—and she'd be charged as my *accessory.*

And now a mob was hollering in the street,
"Come down, Mrs. Taylor!"
And someone was pounding on the door
—with what must have been a club or two-by-four.
There were more than a hundred voices—
chanting out of cadence—
whistling and howling
till they made my skin slink down my spine.
I had no place to hide myself
—no way to escape the mayhem
they clearly had in mind.
I took the pitcher from its bowl on the dresser
and meant to hurl it
at whoever was the first one through my door.
Someone rapped and shook the handle.
I made out Russell's voice above the roar:
"It's Carry Nation with a crowd in tow
—and the whole press corps from Buffalo and Toronto

—and even two reporters from New York,
who've been assigned to cover all she does
—and now she's come to call on *you*."

[ CARRY NATION ]

When I opened my door,
Russell was halfway down the landing—
with one foot on a step,
and his head rolling this way and that,
like a chained hound who's caught an irresistible scent
and wants to be untied so he can run.
I smoothed my dress and told him not to hurry me—
Carry Nation meant nothing to me.
She was standing in the foyer, with a dozen men around her,
and more outside the door
—and the door wide open,
and all of late October blowing in!
*What did she want?—*
*I'd read all about her "hatchetations"—*
*and here was a mob, howling for action*
*—and I could see the axe, held casually in her hand,*
*the way another woman might have held a parasol.*

Then Russell, with his winks and three-ring patter,
coaxed the crowd to move outside—
and asked them to "pipe down
for the sake of the tender ladies."
After he'd shut the door,
he ushered the reporters to the parlor,
and introduced us with his flourishes
—as if it were a title bout:
"Two Titanesses," he called us!
(and the dutiful reporters wrote it down).

Then Carry Nation leaned forward in her chair
and began to speak about her mission:
God had summoned her to Buffalo, she said,
for the Pan American Exposition—
whose "idle and inebrious crowds"
might be saved by her "fulminations"
(which is what she called her sermons).

"And why are you taking your dangerous course of action?"
she asked—with such solicitousness—
that it was obvious she had designs on me.
So I raised my guard—
not only for the hatchet (which had vanished in her cape),
but for any other tactics she might use.
I had read a book about her—
I knew what to expect when "the frenzy" seized her.
And I recalled how she'd been beaten by her husband—
a drunken preacher—
after she stood up at his service
—and corrected his sermon line by line.
I remembered that her mother spent her lifetime
convinced that she was Queen Victoria
(the family slaves were forced to bow as if to royalty!).
And she had an aunt who believed she was a weather vane!
(It's all in her biography.)

And now I was sitting knee-to-knee with her—
"The Kansas Cyclone"—in a boarding house parlor!
And I needed no weather vane
to tell me which direction she was taking:
she had come to take over my enterprise.
So I plugged up every opening against her.
I was in this alone.

I wanted no sponsor—
no *stowaway!*—
*no one's mission* dragging me down
as I barreled to the brink.
I knew if she found a chink, she be in in a minute,
carving her slogans on my ribs—
or she'd make her way down to the dock,
with that heckling crowd at her heels—
to see her smash a flask of rum against my lid
—and launch me into the stream of *her publicity.*

I wanted her gone. I stood up and made apologies,
explaining that I'd be *"traveling"* in the morning—
and that night I needed rest.
She rose too—to her six-foot height,
extended a gloved hand and wished me well.
And I saw, level with my eyes,
a silver hatchet pinned to her lapel.
I strained to see the portrait on its shaft—
like a emperor on a coin—but with spectacles and a bonnet!
And seeing me so, she undid the clasp
and laid it in my hand: "I usually sell these for a quarter,
but wear it in the morning for God's blessing—and my own.
And if it brings you grace,
I know you'll think of some way to repay me."
I didn't see her to the door—
but when I heard the roaring fade,
I tossed her graven image in the grate.

# III

## THE DESCENT

A crowd flowed onto the Suspension Bridge.

Another onto Prospect Point.

A third onto the Three Sisters Islands

—and all along the railings in the gorge.

Across the river, a thousand more poured down to Table Rock.

And up the shore, a hundred others—

men, women, and children—

stood by the dock at Truesdale's cottage, waiting to see me off.

There were no clouds that morning,

and so much light it seemed ten suns were whirling

as I stepped into the skiff—in a tossing sea of handkerchiefs—

and waved to them (while Russell blew a kiss)

amidst the general hurrah.


Then we set out—with Truesdale straining the tiller

against the single, headstrong sail—

and Billy Holleran, a strong, strapping boy, manning the furious oars.

The barrel rode upright behind us, bucking to run its course

—and was jerked back to correction by the stern instruction of our rope.

A quarter way out, we stopped on an island where I changed my clothes:

no hat or dress now, but a blouse left open at the throat,

and a skirt hemmed just below the knee.

I made them turn away while I backed in through the rim—

then they fastened down the lid,

rolled me to the shore,

turned me upright—

pushed me in.


Four boats now. And behind the first,

the towed barrel, weighed down with me—

yet still intractable.

And in the last, a cameraman recording every stroke

as they rowed a mile across to the Point of No Return—
where the river starts to churn,
and a sailor knows he'd better bend his back
—or else go over.
There they knocked. And cut the rope.
They must have pulled hard then to turn themselves south,
but I went north—(a half mile more before I'd reach the brink).
I careened and spun. Once it tossed me clear up out of the water.
I went unbidden—and unwelcome—where it rushed me.

I wished I could have watched from some place overhead
and heard the voices racing down the shore—
passing on the message—
dock to island, island to rock, rock to bridge:
"She's coming!"
I would have liked to see them turn their heads—
wave after wave, as each new group heard the murmur
and craned their necks to catch a glimpse.
I'd have liked to see the trolley racing down the shore,
and the incline railway rushing down the gorge—
so the ones who'd waved from Truesdale's dock
could be standing on the rocks below the Falls,
looking up—to see if anything would come.

[ DESCENT ]

Over the Horseshoe's lap I dropped
—through the watery shrouds that clung about its knees.
It rolled me over and grasped me in its jaws
and was determined to have me.
My neck was lashed. My brain tore.
I felt it skin me like a hare.
Its fingers settled on my throat,
and had it asked me

to surrender to its roar
of blackness, its blaze
of nothingness,
I'd have yielded
for any drop
of mercy.

Then I glimpsed, through the turbulence,
my father and mother who had died when I was twelve.
Once I mourned them beyond recovery,
and here they were—signaling me to come.
And there was my young husband—
dead since I was twenty—
and in his arms,
our baby—
trembling and whimpering
—as on the day he left me.
I wanted to go with them.
I wanted to console them.
I wanted them
to save me.

But then I fell into the whirlpool,
and my veins and arteries unwound.
My cord rocketed from its stack of bones.
My joints unlatched. My pulse
spread out through space. Every atom of me
dispersed—to a place I couldn't name.
I moved in and out of it like breath—
expanding and contracting
through its infinite rings,
until only a single
cell of me remained

and dropped
like a pebble
to the bottom.

[ RETURN ]

Awakening in that dark,
where maybe nothing was,
what an effort it took
to keep conscious of the task of being.
Everything around me was shifting
—every surface, wet and slippery—
each motion I made
was a new one:
uncertain and imprecise,
rehearsed and repeated
until I got it right
and could keep going.
Once I slipped, and, falling,
was certain I heard something whimpering.
I pushed myself toward it
—stumbling headfirst over things
that groped
to stay me as I passed.

Finally, where the water ended,
something soft spread itself before me,
and I might have stopped and slept forever
—if a crack of light hadn't broken through then
—and nudged me forward
—to push myself through
before it closed again.
It was narrow. It hurt. It seemed impossible—
until I saw the child,

lying with her knees up to her chin.
I worried she was dead
because I'd come so slowly.
I bent to stroke her hair
—and felt my fingers
cradling my own head.
And so—
I brought myself
to life.


[ DEBRIEFING ]

Sealed in my barrel,
I was awakened by a jolting flash of light
as something hurled me from the whirlpool
—and I saw a hand
(moving beneath the monogrammed initial on my cuff).
And when its fingers floated down and touched my skull—
I felt a throbbing pulse—I knew I was *alive!*
And though I tossed on for an hour—
afraid that I would die—
in the hellish cauldron below the Falls
—already I'd been saved:
I had gone into the grave and found *myself* there.
So I waited (and I prayed)
till the thunder snapped again
—and someone snagged a strap
and dragged me in.

At first they couldn't budge the lid—
I was frantic, gasping, breathless
—someone ran to get a saw—
then everyone was shouting, "She's alive!"
The church bells rang as I took a wobbly step.

Their hands reached out to touch me.
A child ran to hug me—but her mother pulled her back.
They started to inspect me: was I "launching a crusade?"
A woman yelled, "Your mother must be spinning in her grave."
Then Russell stepped forward and gave the crowd a wave,
and handed me a single red carnation.
Now reporters asked for "detailed observations."
(A preacher wanted "secret revelations.")
They didn't *know* what to do with me
—And I had thought
that they would *praise* me.

I was hurt. I was cold. I said I wanted to go home.
And when their brief "elation" had slumped to disappointment,
they brought me to my bed,
piled on the blankets,
and wedged hot water bottles, up and down my sides.
I lay as still as a cadaver, grateful for the rest
—until a trio of surgeons
began to probe my torso (maybe looking for a gash
to put their hands in—so they could prove, as in the gospel,
that I truly *was* alive).
They flexed and poked me for an hour
(at least they didn't use their knives),
they gave me plasters, ointments, pills
—left a little stack of bills—
and pronounced me "fit"—
for the reporters.

Already jotting, they took their places at three sides of my bed—
flattering me, coaxing me to speak,
and when the words refused to come,
one brought his head close to my cheek

and whispered, "We're all in this together now."
But how could I explain what I'd found below Niagara—
how I saw my soul in slumber
—how I struggled for its life.
So I described instead—
how I bumped across the rapids,
and how I tumbled down the Falls:
"And as you see," I said, "I'm still alive."
But when I read their faces, all I saw was disappointment.
And at last I understood what they had wanted,
but by then I'd gone too far to change my story
—and tell them I was dead.


[ VANDALS ]

A sound—
Wood creaking?—
Footsteps!—(Moving slowly down the floorboards in the hall).
Quiet again
—and then, outside my door—a whispering.
Now and then some words came through:
"Dammit," or "I'm telling you."
It was Russell, arguing, "Go in. Go in!"
And in came Caroline,
turning her reluctance into brisk, maternal cheer—
inquiring how I felt—had I slept well?
Could I tell if I was "fit enough to walk"—
or "talk to Tussie about some offers from New York?"
And without waiting for an answer or a nod,
she pulled apart the drapes—and let the morning in.

Then she moved on to the news of what had happened
on the dock where they'd moored my barrel for the night.
Half the people of Niagara had come down for souvenirs.

*41*

They cut my harness into strips,
ripped off the leather straps,
pried out the iron bolts
(the lid was lost at once
—but even its broken hasp had been unscrewed).
Now everyone had a splinter—
everyone had a sliver of the barrel I had made—
that I'd sketched out on my knees,
that I'd fitted to my shape—
that had taken me where no one had ever gone before
—they were selling *me* in pieces,
and Caroline was amused.

She described—how (when every strippable thing was stripped),
the late ones crawled inside
—and carved their names with penknives in my ribs.
But she told me not to worry:
her Tussie had gone out
(when it got light) "and chased them all away."
No, I needn't worry—
her Tussie had "everything in control":
The barrel was already being fixed—
he'd ordered a new lid
—"A few new straps and a harness,
and no one will ever know the difference."
She poured some water from my pitcher
and drank it down herself
—and asked if I was starting to feel better.

[ THE TRIUMPHAL PROCESSION ]
Two million lights glowed on the daylit streets
of the Pan American Exposition.
The Grand Army of the Republic was on hand—

and everywhere, a military band, with braided epaulets and shakos,
marching by in regimented rows.
People had assembled from all points of the globe—
a whole village of Eskimos—
and the Royal Mexican Artillery.
I saw ladies in ornate prams
with liveried chauffeurs, who held their parasols aloft—
and rolled them about—like overgrown babies!


There were temples and palaces and Venetian canals
—with tanned, mustachioed gondoliers.
Matadors, flashing crimson from their capes
—and menacing Cossack riders—
galloping by with swords and bandoliers.
My carriage rolled through miles of satin bunting,
past garlanded fountains,
under arches of gleaming electric lights
—and finally crossed the triumphal bridge
—with its towering columns—where four marble stallions
reared up in the directions of the wind.


I was expected to be regal there. But all I longed to do
was sleep. My shoulder ached. And my scalp
throbbed beneath my spray of feathers.
It was late October and so cold I took the blanket from the coach—
and dragged it up the platform—
where I was expected to pose,
exposed to the weather, and greet the endless crowds.
—For hours they came—jostling from the distance
and finally tapering into line—
an ocean slowly trickling through a funnel
—and I had to tap each drop before it fell!

I held a cat, a stand-in for the one who'd drowned.
It warmed my lap, and several people
stooped to pet its ears
—even if they wouldn't meet my eyes!
At first I tried to give my hand to them,
but then withdrew it, explaining that my shoulder ached,
and asking that they please forgive me.
When they spoke, their words seemed garbled,
especially their names—which was what they mainly told me—
as if I'd become a repository
for fame and immortality.


Whatever else they said, I can't remember.
I'm certain most of it was kind.
But I was tired beyond all imagining,
and when I raised my eyes, I saw—a thousand more in line.
Occasionally I left my chair and hurried to the Temple of Music,
which had a cast iron stove—
where I tried in vain to thaw my frozen feet.
Some of them objected: "We come all the way
from Bradford to see 'er. She's got an obligation!"
By the evening, they were coming drunk and rowdy,
and found me an easy target for their fun:


One of them shouted to the crowd,
"If they had left it up to me, I would've left her in that barrel."
And another (even drunker), spotting some friends in line,
called out: "Don't waste your time—it's Methusaleh's wife!"
I watched as he moved on with them
—probably to the next pavilion—behind whose gilded sign
was "Señorita Bonita, the Naughty Spanish Dancer."
Or maybe to stare at the bloody spot outside the Temple of Music

where McKinley had been shot the month before
—and nothing I had done
was able to compete with *that.*

That night as I left the Exposition,
I couldn't help but see (in the glow of the electric lights),
that Indian maiden—"the Maid of the Mist."
She was naked and slender,
with long brown hair and delicate features
—and in urgent need of rescue
as she plunged from the brink in her oarless canoe.
She was prominent and everywhere—
the symbol for the Exposition
—on handbills—on posters—on banners!
—an available measure to compare me to.
And so I understood what I was up against—
and why everyone, who'd stood in line to meet me,
had met me with the same glazed disappointment
I used to see in children's eyes,
all those years I spent in school
—whenever I would try to teach some truth.


But how easily I could enthrall those same bored children,
by leaving truth behind and opening a book of fairy tales,
where every kingdom had a pretty, sleeping princess.
—And every boy could dream how he would save her
(and every girl resolved to go to sleep!).
"The great Niagara has been conquered by a woman!"
The headlines had given me away,
and now no man (or boy) could save me anymore.
I had thrown away my frailty and my fear—
my most appealing "female traits"

(I had lost my youth and beauty long before)
—now everything about me was a liability.
My old invisibility fell from my face:
I, Annie Taylor, turning gray and thick in the waist,
had dared to do a thing that no man had ever done.
I stood before them like a Gorgon
and turned them into stone.

Yet inside me, something glowed
like a tuft, ripped from the hide
of the golden fleece!
I had gone into the grave to get it—
and after struggling back with it,
I asked only that it be acknowledged—
that my *deed* be acknowledged—
that my *life* be acknowledged.
Yet they dismissed me when I said I was *alive*
—that I was *living* proof
that *they* could do
the thousand things they longed to do but never dared.
I stood before them
with the weeds still tangled in my hair,
and the silt still dripping from my nose—
But no one looked beneath my surface
—to see something that might not repel them.

[ OFFERINGS ]

In the morning, I could hardly lift my head to see the clock,
and when the breakfast bell clanged below,
I sat up, felt the cold and pulled the spread around me.
How could I go down and tell them what I planned?
—that I'd be traveling on the next train back to Michigan.
But having gone so far alone,

46

was it so unreasonable
to ask only *to be left alone again?*
Of course I knew in time there would be bills,
and then I'd have to travel
—maybe for a month or two each spring:
a modest itinerary to a few northeastern cities—
with clubs or universities, that could afford the modest fees
to support the modest life I had planned.

Russell barged into my reverie of my future
—and dropped an inch-high pile of papers on my bed.
He was tired, he said, of my "eternal indecisions,"
he'd just signed "a contract with New York."
We'd be leaving after breakfast
—I could have the details later—
but now he didn't want "a lot of backtalk."
When he left, I started sifting throught the papers—
there were telegrams and letters—
and newspaper clippings with torn, ragged edges.
*Where* were the requests from the universities—
the learned societies—the atheneums?
The only queries were from dime museums—
the only milieu Russell knew.

One offered to install me on their lower level—
beside the amputated leg of a Union Army general.
Another sent a handbill on their "mummified mermaid"
—claiming we'd be "a natural."
But later that night, I rode with Russell and Caroline
in the close compartment of a train—
taking us back to Michigan.
He had tried for hours to wear me down—
to make me rush off to New York

and be the *slow act* on some stage
while they changed the backdrop in a vaudeville show.
"You've got seize the day when the iron is hot!" he cried.
(But not even *Lincoln*
could have made me change my mind.)

# IV

*THE ROAD*

Two weeks after I had stunned the world
—had forced Niagara to pause in its course to regard me—
Two weeks after I'd engraved myself on history
—I sat in a vacant store in Bay City, Michigan,
telling my story for a dime.
For fourteen days, the pieces gathered,
and though the puzzle wasn't yet complete,
it seemed that Russell, with his casual extravagance,
had squandered everything—before we'd even left Niagara!
Everything I'd earned was gone,
and each morning, in the mail, came another dunning note,
and so I sat behind that glass all afternoon
—hardly the sleeping beauty—
more like someone in a pillory
—or a debtor on exhibit in her jail.
I kept the barrel by my side—
refurbished since the vandals had their way with it
(and that had meant *another* bill).
And on my lap, a cat I'd borrowed from my boarding house
—especially adept at keeping still.

I answered *all* their questions—which were all the same:
"What did it feel like?"
"Were you awake?"
"Would you do it again?"
"How much money did you make?"
—and, "Can I pet your cat?"
The cat met its task compliantly:
its eyes would wrinkle up,
and its muzzle twist into any lady's glove.
I, likewise, did my best to oblige them

—man, woman, child—I told it over and over:
described my terror at the icy water pouring in,
the refusal of the hatch, and then my first breath
as the church bells rang on both sides of the river.
Though I never even *tried* to explain what I'd found there
—or what had taken place inside me.
And with every telling, my moment shrunk
—turned physical, replaceable. Sensate and finite.
I put perimeters around it ("beginning" and "ending")
—just a matter of positioning.

What I'd done had once seemed larger than the world
—and now I doled it out in ten-minute intervals
so each of them listening
could dispense it in ten seconds
to the next one in the crowd.
The Falls shrunk as they carried off its pieces
—until it seemed a small, scarred rock,
annoyingly dropped on some farmer's new-plowed field.
I should have known it was not a thing for words.
Maybe a painter could have got it whole,
could have told about the motion and the light,
could have hinted at the moment of creation—
that collision of hell and paradise
—could have said what I felt inside
(and still feel now)
—though I could never find the words for it.
And still I had to tell it. And tell it again. And tell it
tomorrow. And tell it the next day.
And the next week down in Flint
—where Russell had found another empty store.

*Where was all the money?*
I drew up a list and handed it to Russell:
*Where was the money* for my interview
in *Godey's Lady's Magazine?*
For my endorsement
of Gould's Rheumatic Ointment?
For the display of my barrel
in the lobby of the State Park Hotel?
He swore that all of it was spent,
and while he shared my disappointment
—my present predicament was my *own* responsibility.
The two hundred I'd received
for sitting in the cold at the Pan American Exposition
had gone to "our necessities in the Falls
—things like lodging and meals,
trains and carriages—
the blacksmith and harnessmaker."
(I added "tavernkeepers.")


He showed me bills from the rivermen and physicians,
a night nurse and apothecary.
There also were "gratuities"
for the police and the reporters
(as well as a mortician
who'd been "waiting in the wings").
He mentioned some "disbursements" to his wife
—not exactly a salary—
but a small compensation
for her services "as a lady's companion."
Then he asked me, how could I *possibly* complain,
when I was the one who had brought him

"to the brink of wrack and ruin"
with my "sky-high operation
and sudden case of nerves."
And now, "to avoid starvation,"
I must "swallow my pride, and eat humble pie,"
and follow his directions.

A decade later, I was sent, anonymously,
a letter he'd written to the National Geographic Society
on my behalf—
all of it misspelled and ungrammatical
—and so full of bombast
that I had to laugh,
despite the pain he'd brought into my life.
But that first winter, I couldn't grasp
why there hadn't been *one* offer
from any place respectable.
Instead we traveled to Flint and Saginaw
(to a string of empty stores)
—and on to Cincinnati, Sandusky, and Cleveland
(where the stores had "live attractions" in their windows).
And there I sat—
amid canvas spats and bowler hats,
on a fainting couch or a boudoir chair
—or in a pile of "ladies' finery":

I, in my frayed black dress,
with my barrel by my side—
and on my lap, another tame (but shedding) cat
—and all the people filing past,
or coming up to press their lips
—or breathe their foggy circles on the glass.
Some of them stood for ten or twenty minutes

(mouthing words I'm sure their mothers
would have washed away with soap).
Some poked their tongues and rolled their eyes,
the way children do at zoos.
And after they were through,
I'd see them in the basement of the store,
where they sat on folding seats
(with their parcels on their laps)
—tapping their umbrellas on the floor—
as if I were a manikin,
and *they* could make me speak.


[ SOUTH TO SPRING ]

Finally, the earth tipped
—and the sun came like a suitor,
zealous with flowers.
And I moved toward it
across the latitudes
to where the ice withdrew
—and left me surer footing.


Snowdrops found the openings
in the crust.
And crocuses crept slowly from their bulbs.
And in empty fields,
where houses once had stood,
the lilacs poured their fragrance
for the bare foundations.


Then the sky packed up
its coat of winter coal dust,
and one day opened onto a meadow,
where trees were waking

to the trills of rippling brooks
—and geese honked north
above the breaking buds.

At night the courting peepers
rang the ponds,
and in the morning in the woods,
the bloodroot
and the adder's tongues unfurled.
And farther south—where winter never was,
I saw magnolias hung with moss—

and hurried on—
against the course and protests of the geese,
who, flying north
at such great height
and at such speed,
couldn't see—though I waved it at their wings—
that I finally had a contract in my hand.

[ THE SOUTHERN EXPOSITION ]

Two dozen riders standing on stallions
bore a canopy of garlands down the center of the midway.
Behind them, a bevy of lithesome young beauties
leaned from gold ladders on chariots and waved.
What a great display of flesh they made
—(I swear I saw a prize potato
with a ribbon wider than their costumes!).
Last autumn's apples had their ribbons too
—as did last summer's pickles,
and the rosy jars of waxy-headed jams,
the strings of sausages and onions,
the bags of cheeses and smoked hams.

And though it was much smaller than its bow,
I saw a single Georgia peanut with seven nuts inside,
lounging on a tiny satin throne.


There was a hall with a bearded lady and hairless man
(and a hall with a sword-swallower and a fire-eater).
A hall where Hawaiians "danced and played banjos"
(and a hall where black men "played banjos and danced")
—And a hall, where a village of Eskimos
(the very ones I'd seen in Buffalo)
stood silent—hot—and motionless.
There was a man who had no arms or legs
—in a shed with a four-winged duck.
At one end, was "Plucky, the World's Smallest Pony,"
at the other was "Lucky, the World's Smallest Horse."
There was a hall with a recreated train wreck:
"See bloody bodies strewn along the track!
—So natural," the pitchman called,
"that you can almost hear them scream."


There were pig races, dog races, three-legged races
And a famous troop of clowns—portraying comic types:
"A policeman and a tramp"—
"A Dutchman and a Hebrew"—and "A woman."
In the evenings, there were waltz and concert bands,
and a man who sailed the dance floor
on a sparkling, mirrored globe—
and, for the highlight of the show,
there was a woman cut in half.
To bring the entertainments to a close,
a seal climbed up a ramp
and tooted "Goodnight Ladies" on his rubber-headed horns.

And every day, until I heard that seal applauding his own song,
I stood beside my barrel in a little clapboard "temple,"
putting on my "act" for anyone who'd come.

[ THE WOMAN-CUT-IN-HALF ]
    The Woman-Cut-in-Half came to my room,
her left eye bruised and her lip swollen,
trembling as she told me
that her husband was asleep
so it was safe for her to talk now:
"What he does out there—in the middle of the floor—
is only lights and mirrors. And a pretty helper
—you've seen her legs.
But the idea of cutting me in half
has seized his brain—
with that same depraved excitement
that buzzes through the crowd.

"Later—when he's gotten very drunk,
he likes his private game—
telling me how *every* man
would like a woman-cut-in-half—
so he could toss away
her head—and keep the rest
—(with the part that men like best—between her legs).
And with me on the bed, he does his pantomime—
laying the sharp saw on my belly, pressing it gently
—it's all a game, you see—all of it lighthearted—
as long as I keep still. And if I don't,
it's my own fault that he has to use his fists.

"After years of holding still—with all those lights
and everyone's eyes—and all their heavy breathing

—and the crazy sound of his sawing,
it should be easy to lie there in that room with him.
Sometimes I pretend I'm something else—
like an old forest—with a tree cut down each night
—till there's not much left to worry about.
He's right, I should be happy to hold still—
when *he's* the one
who makes our arrangements
and pays all our bills
—and all *I* have to do is *lie there.*


" 'It's an easy role,' he says—
'and natural for a woman.'
He's right, of course: you *never* see a man
get sawed in half—(it's *always* a woman—on her back).
And in the morning, I can see that he's ashamed.
He brings me coffee. And squeezes
my shoulder so tenderly
—that I could forgive him then with all my heart.
But when he sees these marks he's made himself,
it sets him off again—
shouting how ugly I've become—
how I'm ruining his act."


[ THE COMING OF THE HERO ]
For two weeks I stood in my "temple"
(a shed, decked out in classical revival),
but I was no goddess from antiquity
—just a woman of this century,
trying to tell my story,
and dispense whatever wisdom they'd accept from me.
There were fifty folding chairs spread out before me
—and gaslights blazing day and night

because there were no windows.
I lectured every hour on the hour,
and Russell (who'd arrived without his wife)
would start barking half an hour before the show.
He'd had a banner made in Cleveland
by a man who'd never seen me.
It showed a bow-lipped girl with golden curls,
holding a scepter
as she plunged over Niagara
in a gilded barrel that skimmed
her rounded breasts.
*"Educational and Inspirational!"*
was painted above her head
—so the women towing children
would come in.

There I'd wait behind my dressing screen
(beside my latest cat)
—and count the sets of footsteps
that came scraping to the seats.
"Ten minutes till the show!"
I'd hear Russell through the doorway
—with twenty minutes to go.
He kept my barrel beside him on the midway as a draw.
And when it was time, he'd call some passerby
and offer him a ticket if he'd help him roll it in.
When I'd hear the barrel rumbling,
I'd get ready for his flourishing introduction.
Then I'd step out on the platform and don my leather straps,
and, using the cat, would demonstrate
how I once crawled in that barrel
—backwards through the rim.
Then I rushed them through the rapids—

I bumped and whirled them—
I led them to the brink—
and let them drop.
I closed my eyes while I wove their spinning terror in the dark.
Then my saw cut through the lid—
and gave them light.

I spoke with all the dignity I could muster in that place—
sharing every shred of courage that remained in me
—offering every word of hope
that they could take back to their lives
and wield against their daily human miseries.
But as I spoke, I noticed their confusion:
they had come to see that golden-headed girl,
full of carefree callow pride,
trembling in her barrel
till the God of Fortune smiled and let her go.
They wondered *who* I was—
And *why* I had her place
(I heard children ask their mothers when she'd come).
And one night as I began,
I watched a tipsy man
stagger up to ask me
*Was I Queen Victoria?*
(I couldn't answer through the laughter he had roused.)
And then a chill set in,
moving swiftly, mouth to mouth,
striking the crowds before they were halfway
down the midway
—saying, it was wisest to avoid me.

One night ten tickets sold. And the next night,
only three. And one evening, after waiting

what seemed hours for the rumbling of my barrel
—after I'd smoothed my hair and brushed the cat,
and still could hear no sound
—I stepped out from behind the dressing screen
and found there was no one there.
(Not even Russell
—who'd left the barrel in the back and disappeared.)
A concussion of applause
came toward me from the distance,
and I tracked its aftershocks across the midway—
through a throng around the doorway
of a new exhibit.
I pushed my way inside
and saw that every chair was taken.
And in one of them, sat Russell—
shouting and clapping with the rest—
as a burly man in an open shirt with scars across his chest,
stood brandishing a knife and sipping from a flask—
to dramatize—
how he'd wrestled down a grizzly
*"to save a woman's life!"*


[ CRAWL ON ALL FOURS ]
Please don't misunderstand me:
not for *one* moment did I expect the kind of accolades
that belonged to those who'd reached the Pole,
or found the Nile's source,
or the cure for some disease
or large-scale human misery.
But I was a heroine—even if a minor one—
by any definition.

I was the *only* one who'd taken on Niagara—
a test of human will—
a feat the whole world said,
no man will *ever* do
—And so I kept a naive hope
that *someone* might want to hear my story.

In every city—every town with a tent—
crowds lined up daily to listen to the men
who could tell them how it was
to swim the Channel—
or explore the jungle
—or spend a week on a flagpole in a field!
There was a man at the Exposition
who was getting nightly raves
for describing how he'd
lived inside a cave for half a year
(his wife brought him his meals and did his laundry),
and through his silence and discipline,
he had found the *fourth* dimension
—and everyone was lining up to hear him.

There was another who had dangled from a plane
that dropped him chained and blindfolded
into the ocean! And a man who claimed
he'd died and gone to heaven
where he recognized several friends—
and a host of prominent people,
who sang the *most unusual* hymns
—which he still could hum
(even though a doctor had revived him).
Russell praised their strategies

—all that poppycock and derring-do—
and their costumes and their scenery
(some of it quite costly)—and mused about
their managers' shares of revenue.

Then one evening during dinner in the canteen,
he pointed out a man,
who had crossed the Brooklyn Bridge
—by walking up its girders on his hands.
The man sat down beside us
(it struck me this was planned)
and told me that he'd been to see my show—
And if I'd take "some kind advice,"
he could "blow a little life" into my act.
He'd suggested I should add some song and dance:
he'd composed a tune himself—
on the Brooklyn Bridge, of course
—but for "a small reward,"
he'd set it with some words about the Falls.

And if my legs still had "some shape,"
I should hike my skirt and pantomime my fear:
He rolled his trousers
up his calves to help him demonstrate
—then let go—*a shrill falsetto*
(that stunned me so I couldn't even laugh).
"I've been thinking," Russell said, as if on cue,
"then she should get down on all fours—
and crawl into her barrel
—and tell her tale from there."
And everyone around us
(with their elbows on the table,
and their supper in their mouths)
nodded to endorse this *grand idea*.

Next morning—not a trace of Russell,
and it was easy to assume he'd gotten drunk
—(it's what he did each night after our rows)
and it was nice to picture him hungover now—
with a throbbing head
that might keep throbbing well past nine
—when he should have been arriving
at the temple with the key!
*Was this his childish way of getting back at me?*
He knew the show was scheduled for ten—
that I needed time (to change my dress
and arrange my props). The barrel
and the cat were locked inside—I heard the cat let out a cry
when I tried to pry the hasp with my metal comb.

I kept fiddling with the lock till half past nine—
saying words I'd never said before in public
—and I said them all the way to the men's dormitory—
where I rang and rang the bell—
and when no one came, I said, "To hell
with propriety!" and climbed a flight of stairs
to a room of rumpled beds, where an old clown
raised his head—and waved for me to come,
calling, "Sweetheart," "Darling," "Dearie"—
and a litany of other "pretty things" I couldn't hear
since I was stumbling down the stairs—
and dashing down the midway—
where I ran into
the Woman-Cut-in-Half.

She brought her husband with his wooden
case of hacksaws (he impressed me
with the deftness of his hands)

—And when the shaft split and the lock fell,
I pushed against the door, and daylight crossed the floor—
to the stage where my barrel should have been!
The cat came rubbing on my shins
—where was its cage?
—And the penny picture postcards that I sold at every show?
—Behind the screen, I found the *empty* coin box.
So now, after all I'd done to avoid it,
all the lengths I'd gone to—even over Niagara—
I went to the office of public relief
and begged for *charity*.


Someone made arrangements for a ticket to Niagara
(where a benevolent society agreed to take me in).
And there, in the months that followed,
I learned that Russell had gone north
and had adapted my act:
Employing another cat, he'd stand beside my barrel
and tell his audiences how he'd been my "lifelong friend"
—*how I'd been his teacher once!*—
and how, when I asked for his assistance with my plan,
he had tried to dissuade me
—but finally agreed to manage me
*only in order to protect me.*
He told them how he'd designed the barrel himself
*sparing no expense—as my safety was at stake.*


And though, he claimed, I'd broken *several bones*
(he gave them extra gore—the way they liked),
I survived the ordeal—thanks in large part to his bravery.
He pantomimed the way—
when he saw me trapped inside the whirlpool,
he threw off his coat—*and with no thought for his life—*

66

swam out into the rapids, grabbed a strap,
and, kicking on his back, towed my barrel in.
He showed them how he pried the lid
to give me back my breath,
then lifted me out gently—
*the way he once held his own dying mother—*
and how (with my arms around his neck)
—I kissed him in my gratitude.

# V

## THE QUEST

Now imagine a scenario
—imagine you're a boarder in a small house in Niagara,
when the postman rings the bell.
And though nothing worth a glance has come for months,
this morning there's an envelope for you,
and it allows you a quickening of hope—
a tiny dab of fragrance on the pulse
—because, for once, someone might want you.
It's only an ounce of paper,
but it's logged five hundred miles
till it's finally in your hand.
And as you rip the wax seal from its flap,
a clipping shows, and you pull it out—
reading as you pull,
and your heart is beating—
because you're reading your story
—though it's not about *you* at all.


It's been sent "for your comments"
(by a reporter in Chicago)
since it tells the *central story of your life*
—which suddenly belongs to someone else!
So now you know just how I felt
—I'd been *erased*—
and in my place, "an actress would be cast"—
she would be "young and beautiful"
(the words were underlined),
and to requite her (for *my* sufferings!),
she would find the "happy ending" that eluded me.
*Who were these people in my place?*
Who was this "pleading heroine" in my barrel?

—and this "villainous husband"—who'd "set me adrift"
where my own free will had taken me?
And how did this "handsome sailor in a skiff,"
get to *save me* from the whirlpool?

I had *saved myself—by myself*
—and now I could not *find myself* in my *own* story!
But as I read further, I came to Russell's name:
He claimed he'd been "commissioned by a theater,"
and now a play *"about me"* was heading to the stage.
"Always happy to oblige the public,"
he offered to display my barrel
"for an undisclosed fee—
and a guarantee that a role for him
would be written in the play."
(Knowing Russell,
he would probably insist on playing *me!)*
My barrel could be viewed outside the theater,
and every hour on the hour, Russell would be on hand
—to answer any questions and bring the crowds inside,
where they could have what they'd always wanted:
my story—pat and pretty—and *without me.*

[ GRAIL QUEST ]

Now every day, I had to think about my barrel
being forced to authenticate that travesty.
No, it wasn't Moses' basket. Or the Ark
—or even Keats's urn. But it was genuine. And mine—
sturdy, country oak—original growth—
and it had delivered me from a drafty floor in Michigan
—where my flesh had tingled
as I traced around my shape to make its pattern.
Wasn't it *my skin—my womb—my child?*

And being so, I couldn't bear to see it standing in the cold
while Russell bragged about it
like some barroom Lothario!

—I couldn't bear to see the smirks of passersby,
running their hands along my sides,
commenting on my shape,
or laughing while some raffish one
rubbed his crotch against the wood
—or kissed his finger and bent halfway over—
to stroke the bottom where I'd crouched.
I couldn't stand their matches flaring up—to look for blood.
I couldn't bear their knocking on the staves—
calling me names and summoning me to come—
as if I were a genie who'd ascend from some far place
to do their bidding.

And worst of all was their shouting—
*shouting!*—till the whole thing rang with their voices
—echoing out of the emptiness
because I wasn't there.
And day upon day, as I listened to a hundred hoots and catcalls,
it drowned my power to speak.
And I saw I'd have to go there—to bring my barrel home.
I had to lean myself against its imperturbable, thick sides—
and touch that rim again
—where I'd circled my finger
a thousand times—to help me tell my story.
Wasn't it *my voice—my truth—my talisman?*

But *how* could I rescue it?—I was destitute—
rooming in the back room of a boarding house,
where I cooked and cleaned and fetched for "working" men.

But then an inspiration came, I labored with my pen,
and later—from a stall (outside a shop in Niagara Falls),
I sold copies of my memoir for a dime.
When my jar was full, I contacted a lawyer
—who put a private detective on the case.
Paying his retainer, I was skeptical at first.
But then "a lead" emerged:
he'd seen a barrel in a store
—to promote a revival of that play.

I was instructed by my lawyer to journey to Chicago
—and book my train and lodgings under "two fictitious names."
And though I bristled at the cloak-and-dagger
claptrap of his game, I was swept into its spirit
and played my part with relish.
I played the "primary witness"
when my barrel was seized by the police
(above the protests of Russell
—and the managers of the theater and the store).
And next morning, I was sitting on a train,
heading back to Niagara,
and I had my barrel—and my *voice* again.

[ *THIS* WAS THE MAN ]

Recovered now—my voice—my *life!*
—and all those machinations and anxieties behind,
and Russell gone forever, I vowed that this time
(when I chose a manager)—I'd be as careful as I'd been
in cutting out the pattern for my barrel:
I'd try him first—I'd seek compatibility of nature—
decency and common sense,
some delicacy of manner,
and I'd insist on references

that would speak to his morality and honor,
his reliability and diligence,
and I'd require some evidence of superior intelligence—
plus a few particularities about his recent client history
(and a bit of testimony on the matter of sobriety)
—as well as a sample of his grammar.

I made discreet inquiries
and was referred to a local government official,
who had a brother—("a theatrical promoter"
—not some amateur purveyor of adolescent stunters!). He also
was a bachelor. (William Banks was his name.)
From his office in Ohio, he sent a three-page résumé,
full of dates and names that showed how he'd arranged
the Midwest bookings of Paderewski and Caruso
(and other virtuosos, whose names I didn't know).
And in the personal note that was attached,
he detailed (quite grammatically)
the itinerary he'd set for Ellen Terry
("and several other lovely leading ladies")
—as well as his "recent difficulties"
on a lecture tour he'd booked for G. B. Shaw.

*This* was the man! It heartened me to note
that his command of the language nearly matched my own.
And, warmed by his candor,
I sent a letter, disclosing my sad history with Russell
—and the complexities of traveling with a barrel
(I didn't want him to be so rosy-eyed that he'd overlook
the considerable expense and exceptional accoutrements
that were attendant on a venture like my own).
In reply, he enclosed his photograph,
which showed him to be a gentleman—

with a touch of grey and a handsome smile,
which I returned unreservedly—
when I came to his assurance
that I could "rely" on him completely
—and would soon "have the chances I deserved."

He promised, in the fall, I'd be lecturing at universities
and for learned societies in New York
(where he had family ties and school connections):
"But, given your credentials, we mustn't hang about
like a pair of rusting rakes
—when now, in every state,
there are regional, national, and international fairs
that would be *thrilled* to have you in their schedules."
And so I went with him that summer:
always lecturing on time—and displaying my barrel
in good electric light—and never being asked
to demean my message (with a foolish pantomime).
And night after night, he tallied up our earnings,
and in the morning, took a portion to a bank
("so it might thank us for its keep").

And week after week, he gave me an allowance
—just as he might have done, had I been his wife.
And by summer's end, for the first time in my life,
I had enough to keep in the gloves in my dresser
(different denominations in the different colored pairs
—just the way my mother once had done).
Now and then he had to ask me for a bit of it
for some extraordinary expense—
he might, for instance, require "a gentleman's wardrobe"
to represent me in New York, or to reserve in advance,
accommodations for our anticipated engagements

at Cooper Union and Carnegie Hall—
both of which, he explained,
required an "appearance security"—a cash guarantee—
which I gave to him most willingly.

Then one September morning, he didn't come to breakfast.
And as I sat alone at "our" table,
a feeling of worry crept over me
till I asked the hotel manager
to take me up the stairs to Banks's room—
where the door fell open—on an empty closet
—where I knew his clothes had been.
His trunk was gone—so were the boxes of my memoirs
—(though he'd left behind the postcards with my picture).
And, remembering a scene from the Southern Exposition,
I ran past the manager—down the stairs and through the kitchen—
to the unlit storeroom where my barrel had been kept.
I batted at the air—*it wasn't there!*—
I groped around the dark—And heard the darkness *howl*
when I told it to come out.

[ REMATCH ]

I had opened up the void—that, all that summer,
had been swirling about my heels,
laughing under its breath—
as I went through my motions—like someone treading water,
believing since I'd stayed afloat an hour,
my struggling would be noticed
—and somehow I'd be saved.
But now from that storeroom, a gust broke,
and I knew the wind had changed
—and breakers began to roll—piling on top of each other
as they scrambled up the stairs behind me.

Even as I strained to shut my door against them,
a wave reached up and knocked me to my face
—and held me down, while the rollers piled on—
ripping off my dress, and carrying off my limbs
—every part I might have used
to grasp some mooring.
As the water climbed—and climbed—I watched the dresser tip
and saw the pitcher drift away—with all my breath inside—
For when the mirror floated down, it let me see
my lips were blue,
and there were two gaping pools
where there should have been my eyes.
And when I tried to touch them,
I could only feel *the void.*
All the while, the water rose—
murmuring sounds I couldn't understand
—until taking me for deaf, it spelled itself out
with poundings and whirlings,
and then I recognized—*it was Niagara,*
and I knew it had come back
to challenge me again.

And shouldn't I have expected it would follow me
and *demand* to have a rematch?
Hadn't I gone across the country that summer,
demeaning its power
till it could no longer lift its head—
for the shame or fear of finding me at some fair
—telling the farmers' wives *how I'd conquered it?*
Now it held me down—meaning *to drown me good this time.*
But, even though I *knew* it had a right,
I heard a cry escape my throat—
gurgling and insufficient to summon any help.

But even so, I was surprised
—to find the scattered parts of me were fighting for my life.
And then a shard of light slipped through an opening,
and hands were on my limbs,
lifting me up, and carrying me aloft,
and I thought *I must have beaten down the Falls again.*
There was no sound yet—no *hurrahs* or rejoicings—
no bells ringing hill to hill
—till the clouds above me whirled like wheels
at seeing me alive.
Now from a distance,
I watched as they arranged my limbs.
And though I couldn't yet recall my name or face,
or what I was, or where I'd been,
I could hear them whisper things
like "madness" and "disgrace."
And I came to understand that this time
I was no celebrity,
but an object of their fear and pity.
And their one priority
was to see me *gone.*

[ MAGGIE KAPLAN ]

As soon as I was able to stand up
and wash myself a bit
—and sip a little broth
(without dribbling down my chin),
the hotel manager came in and handed me three bills:
one was mine, another was for Banks,
the third for Maggie Kaplan.
—*Who* was *Maggie Kaplan?*
From his vague description,

I formed a picture of a woman I'd seen many times that week—
show after show (dime upon dime!)—
always in a seat in the row nearest the stage,
listening *so* intently while I spoke.
She had told me how my bravery
had saved her "from the brink of self-destruction"—
how I'd made her think
that "even a woman like herself"
—facing "the greatest obstacles"—
could take her fate into her hands
—and make "somebody" of herself.
(I didn't know she meant
"somebody else.")

And now she had accomplished her objective
—though when she said it,
I wondered what her "obstacles" might be,
seeing how young and pretty she was,
and thinking how well she spoke
—as if she'd had an education—
and I guessed she must have been
"in trouble" with a man.
And so I viewed her with sympathy
—not as a disciple, but a timid pupil
who needed my convincing
that she would someday find a role for her potential
—despite the details of her "private history."
And I let the idea flatter me—
that *I* was to be the agency of her deliverance.
I consciously addressed myself to her
as she sat there at my feet,
memorizing my story, my gestures, and my lines
—till she was ready to run off

to the theaters of New York
with my manager—and my memoirs
—and *become* me.


But the hotel manager,
who stood mumbling with the housemaid by my bed,
pretended shock when I refused to pay their bills.
(He tapped his head to tell the girl
that she was witnessing another lapse of sanity.)
Yet the next day, I dispensed the dollars from my gloves
(to cover my expenses,
and the house calls of the doctors
—and an invoice from a laundress—
which I was too exhausted to contest).
I set enough aside to get me to the station
(where I could pay for half my ticket
—a church group in Niagara would wire down the rest).
And as soon as they could shove me in a dress
and comb the tangles from my hair,
I was headed for the train
with a note pinned on my chest—
telling the conductor
that my "nerves were frayed—"
that I *(who'd defied Niagara!)*
would "require a watchful eye
and careful handling."


[ THE SAME (NEW) ONE ]

A horse clopped over the cobblestones—
I followed its hoofbeats through my window
till it came with cart and cargo
into the funnel of light
that fell from the lamppost on the corner of Front Street.

It was not yet morning
(though I'd been dressed for half the night),
and now with shoes in hand,
I was hurrying out to intercept the cooper
—before he or his helper rang the bell.
I wanted no witness to see what they had brought—
and when I opened the door, I saw a barrel on the cart—
tethered by four strong ropes (it seemed
so full of life and force— they must have
thought it might leap off and roll away).
I touched it with my glove.
I swear *I felt it move.*

And then (baring my hand), I pressed my palm against it
—skin touching skin,
my fingers felt those *"same"* familiar staves.
And in doing so, I miraculously erased
all the thefts and carvings, all the insults and pawings
—every trace of the abuse it had endured during my absence
—all those wounds I'd felt as if they'd burned my skin.
But now those scars slid off as simply
as winter fur in spring.
I stepped back from the wagon
and saw (though it was new) *it was the same one*
—as fresh and virginal
as on the day I'd crawled inside it
—and touched by no one
(aside from the cooper and his helper
—and by the wide Niagara River,
where I'd had it launched *"again"*).

Now the cooper and his helper—
(my unlikely pair of midwives)

rolled it down their ramp—
and stood it up before me on the pavement:
It was glowing—not quite dry
from its annointing in the river.
I gazed on it in silence—as shyly as a bride,
and then (not caring what they thought),
I knelt down and embraced it—and rejoiced to have it home.
Then I asked the men (who shot looks at each other
to say I must be *crazy)*
to roll it, as quietly as they could,
across the flagstones of the alley,
and put it quickly into the closet below the stairs—
which had been waiting half the night
(though it seemed like half my life!)
with a burning light. And an open door.


[ SOLO FLIGHT ]

This time I sought no references or opinions,
but consulting with myself,
I had a sudden (if belated) intuition
—that the *obvious* person—
for the position of my manager
—was *me*.
After the briefest possible interview
(over a breakfast of blueberry pancakes),
I assigned myself the duty
of calling on a scholarly man, much in demand
for his lectures on graphology, phrenology, and hypnotism
(and his solo demonstration of the dance of the honeybee).
Recognizing "my potential"
—and seeing how, as a woman, I would never eclipse him,
he gave me, free of charge, a list of all his contacts
in Boston, Philadelphia, and New York.

And though he said I shouldn't hope
to net the fees he could command
(being a man with a Ph.D. in literature
and a course in natural philosophy),
I could probably—as he had done—
"make a living off the podium."

I started in Boston
where I appeared behind a seven-year-old farm boy,
who, from his prior life in Caesar's army,
could stand and recite *"Omnia Gallia est"*
—up to the part of Vercingetorix's death—
without ever stumbling on a line.
Behind me, came a thirty-year-old woman,
whose spine, "being aligned with the earth's magnetic poles,"
let her read the minds of people in remote parts of the globe
—such as the Emperor of China, who (it seemed)
spent all his nights provoking wars, divining dreams
—and cheating at mah-jongg with his wives.
Last, was an eighty-year-old man,
whose dental plates conducted waves
from Western Union telegrams,
which he rapped out on a table,
while a former government official,
who displayed a letter of testimony
from the late President McKinley,
translated every dash and dot:
COME QUICKLY    STOP
THE CHILDREN HAVE JUST SHOT THE MAID

My audiences were, for the most part, "attentive"
—my act was, by intention, less inventive than the rest:

I adopted a low-key strategy,
using myself as evidence
that common people can confront the greatest obstacles on earth,
and, instead of cowering before them,
should look them in the eye,
and strive to change the world
—or at least their lives.
A few listeners seemed genuinely inspired
(usually these were women, many were wives)
—though others craved more details
on the Emperor's busy nights.
"Just look at *me*," I'd say:
"Small and frail, aren't I proof
that *you* can stand up to the things that frighten or inhibit you,
and do the things you *truly* want to do before you die?
You'll do things so much greater than I did
—and much more *needed* by this world,
and if at times you feel afraid,
then just imagine
that I'm standing by your shoulder."

Then I'd ask them to close their eyes
and *feel* their power—
to feel it flooding through their hearts and their brains:
"And aren't all our brains the same
—whether man's or woman's?
Did nature give you intelligence—
then expect you to hide it,
or let it lie unused?
Is your mind defective? Or do you fail at what you do
because *someone* is standing in your way?"
To end my lecture, I'd lay my hand on my barrel,

and ask them all to rise—
and say along with me, *"I am alive."*
After the applause, there'd often be a few men glowering.
Once, one raised his hand:
"If you're so keen," he asked, "on changing everybody's lives,
why didn't you just make yourself a man?"
Then someone shouted from the rear,
"I met Annie Taylor in New York last year
—a lovely young girl—with pretty blond hair.
Madam, if you have a shred of honor,
you'll admit you're an *imposter!*"

[ IMMUTABILITY CANTO ]
Each winter I lectured in the large cities—
in halls and auditoriums—
in church basements
—and the parlors of wealthy patrons.
Often with hucksters, charlatans, and fabricators.
Sometimes with orators and educators.
—And occasionally with reformers
whose subjects were so serious and urgent
that I yielded them a portion of my time
—giving up an evening's chance to sell my memoirs
(though *every dime* meant my survival till the spring).

It was a grace to realize *(finally)*
that it really didn't matter—half as much as I had thought—
what my listeners said or did.
Let them heckle me. Or walk out in the middle.
But maybe with some luck (either mine or theirs),
a few of them might be moved in some way—
not even remembering who it was—
or what she might have said

that had helped them change the world for the better
(or *at least* had left them more equipped
to deal with the immutable misery of it).

How good, I thought, to be over that fever of old pride
that had made me crave
to be acknowledged for what I'd done.
I felt no loss to find it gone.
And whether it was gone for good, I couldn't say.
But sloshing through the snows of dismal cities
all those winters, I went more easily
once I realized I wasn't dragging it behind me.
And it was comforting to note—that *this* time—
it wasn't taken against my will. I had put it aside myself
—though I couldn't say exactly where or when.

Each night I read for hours in my room,
and I believe my mind improved from it
(though it may sound like vanity to say so).
It was all I asked for now:
to lie with my feet up on a bed, in the company of a book,
and my barrel in the corner
—where I'd paid some boys to bring it on a handcart.
(I'd always find some hungry boys, hanging about after my show,
who for a dime would "roll a barrel
to *a strange, old lady's* room"
—which was always on the ground floor now.)

One night when I couldn't sleep, I rolled my barrel to my bedside,
and laying my cheek against its staves,
tried to feel what I felt inside it on a late October day.
And though I knew I could never return to that place
—*there*—with my face against the wood,

I began to rise on its old buoyancy:
And I saw the sky above me, filled with bright autumnal sun.
And the river, white with spray.
And the sweaty back of the boy who'd rowed
—And this time when he cut the rope,
I heard him wish me well.

And I saw the way I tossed across the rapids—
and how I hurtled down the Falls—
and the way I found myself there
—where it seemed there was no one else.
I saw—*I actually saw it!*— how I whirled inside the void
—where my fingers touched my head to let me know I was *alive.*
But this time in the darkness, I heard a whirring sound—
—I turned around, and now I saw—
the earth was out there too
—Though I knew it couldn't stop to say my name—
as I lay in a dark hotel room, my cheek against its grain.

# VI

## THE GOAL

I would return to Niagara each spring,
when the earth leaned forward, and the days grew warmer
—till one morning, Lake Erie would unlock herself,
and I'd be waiting on the upper river shore
to see her ice floes rushing from the south.
Every place in the hemisphere would be full of breaking buds
—and sturdy tender shoots
exploding through the crust.
But for me, spring *was* the ice
—rushing by without a moment's hesitation,
no hint of terror
as it leapt over the brink:
There were thick slabs of sheet ice, wide as my arms' span
—and shards, scarred with the tine marks of the wind—
Delicate islands of lace-edged shale—
And grey-green frazzil—
as frothy as a field.

And I knew—though I couldn't see the evidence,
that the river was carrying all of us inside it—
all our washed-off cells,
all our sloughed-off skin,
everything wrung out—leached in through the soil
—or dumped deliberately from a porcelain pot!
All of us—being carried down the river,
all of us—across Niagara Falls,
all of us—rushing on through Lake Ontario
—down the the St. Lawrence River
—and into the oceans of the world.
And there, colliding with the cliffs of continents,
mixing our cells with the cells of every other living thing
—and though I couldn't see our dancing,

I could hear a robin's call and the tap of a woodpecker's beak
(the piper's song and the dancer's feet)
—as they leapt to the tune of spring.


[ SUMMER DAYS ]

When summer came,
I'd set myself up on the corner opposite the State Reserve.
I had a clapboard booth with a banner and an awning
—it was as close to the Niagara as they'd let me go.
When it was windy, I would sometimes catch its spray
—and often I would have to raise my voice above its roar.
Sometimes it came rushing up
like a big, excited dog—
shaking off its energy,
jumping on the strangers
who had stopped to speak with me,
and then I'd have to tell it
to be quiet and get down.


In time, the summers parched my hands.
My veins rose and laced among the cracks.
The sun left dappling spots.
And one July, as I signed a picture postcard for a child,
I saw tremors at the tips of my fingers.
(I said, "It's just Niagara
—nudging me to stroke its silly head.")
I learned not to care—when, for a day or two,
no one stopped to ask me *who* I was—or *what* I'd done.
I had tried ten thousand times to tell the world where I had gone.
But I'd never found the words to match its force.
Now I felt most true to it—
when I was able to keep still.

And, despite my body's failures,
*inside,* I was more alive than ever.
And what a pleasure to spend those doldrum days,
dozing in the shade
—with Niagara at my feet—and my barrel by my side.
For her safety, I had her carted home each night,
and in the day, let her rest (beneath a sapling oak
—Like an old woman returning to her roots).
Some days I'd be awakened by a cough,
and someone standing by the barrel would ask me
to describe my position.
Then they'd crouch beside it
and ask me if they had it right.

"Not exactly," I might tell them.
"Put your knees a little closer to your chin
—Like an infant in a womb"
(that would always make the honeymooners blush).
Though it meant most to me
to see someone standing silently—
trying to measure their courage against their fear.
Then I'd say, *"Sure you could—*
I'll even lend you my barrel."
They'd always laugh and walk away,
but I knew already
that Niagara had rubbed off on them,
and who could say where it might lead them?

[ THE SECOND COMING ]

I suppose I was naive not to suspect him.
But I was hardly expecting a rival then
—and with Bobby Leach's subtlety,
I never guessed his purpose or his plan.

*93*

I might have noticed someone obvious
—(someone more like Maggie Kaplan).
But I never thought there'd be a man
who would want to supplant me—
why would *anyone*
want to do what I'd already done?
Even if no one cared very much about it,
I was still "the first to go over Niagara."
(Why would anyone aspire to be "second"?)

Yet from the moment I'd emerged from my barrel,
into the cheering throng on the dock at Clifton Hill,
Bobby Leach was always in my periphery:
a small, thin man—a boaster—loud and vulgar
—smirking in a way that said,
*he'd* always be superior.
And over the years, whenever I returned to lecture in Niagara,
I'd see him standing in the back,
waving his bowler hat (Always a little tipsy).
But those last few summers, I'd begun to see him
on Sunday afternoons, strolling casually in the Reserve,
and only starting over if a group of others
had gathered on the grass around my booth.

Then he'd drift across the street, so nonchalantly,
it seemed he wasn't coming *intentionally* to hear me
—but only happened to be passing by.
If I'd been younger, prettier or richer,
I might have thought I'd caught his eye.
Instead I formed the notion he was drunk
and was enjoying his little prank of annoying me.
I never wondered why he listened *so intently*
while I answered other people's questions

(not once did he ask one of his own):
Could I describe my harness?—Could I show them
how I crouched?—What had I used for buffers?
—And what to weigh me down?


Could I tell him, one man asked,
how the rivermen knew *exactly when* to cut the rope?
By what markings, could they tell "the one safe spot"—
(where a single stream of current
skirts the grim, projecting rocks)?
—So I gave Bobby Leach my blueprint and my map.
But why should I suspect him?
He was only a song-and-dance man
(a local favorite on the vaudeville stage),
and he was agile still, God knows—
So when he finally made his move,
I played the tune, and led him through his steps
—as if we two were waltzing.


He memorized my itinerary
and followed it exactly
—in a barrel, equipped identically to mine—
but made of steel and painted red—with carnival designs!
Still, for all his preparations, all his hubris
(and all the liquor he'd consumed and brought on board),
he came out badly—with shattered kneecaps and a broken jaw.
But he was younger than I,
and mended so well (in so little time!)
that it seemed his footprints were barely dry
before he was on the road, trotting the globe—
and collecting fees that seemed unimaginable
—even in my younger, self-deluding fantasies.

He traveled well—

he was barker, actor, and stuntman in a single tidy package.

And so, no matter where he went

(since he was now the darling of the Falls),

there were constant news reports about him.

And so, despite myself, I followed *his* itinerary

—in England, Scotland, and New Zealand,

where (as the papers told) he did a bit of the old soft-shoe,

then told a few jokes—

before lecturing under a banner that proclaimed that he was:

"Bobby Leach—the *First Man* to go over Niagara."

And no one even *guessed*

there was a *woman* who had gone before him.


[ THE HERMIT OF NIAGARA ]

My legs grew crippled, and my eyes began to fail,

and one morning in July,

I felt so cold—I was certain there'd been frost.

But when a family bought a handful of my cards—

I watched them fan their faces "from the heat."

After they'd gone, I brought one of those cards close to my eyes.

I had to smile that I'd forgotten what they said.

Now it all seemed so farfetched, but I read it anyhow:

"Annie Taylor: the first person to go over Niagara."

And I *remembered* her:

she had been doughty, resolute, and clear-eyed.

Now she trembled in my hand.

I put her down. So she wouldn't fall.


One blustery day, my banner snapped

—I saw it plummeting toward my head

—but just before it struck me,

it suddenly ascended on a gust—thrashing like someone drowning—

and (swept aloft) went scudding for the gorge.
I stood and watched it fall—then sat again to catch my breath.
I must have drifted off
—for suddenly I found—the cat, who kept me company that summer,
was purring on my lap.
I shooed her down—and noticed it was night
—probably well past midnight,
and not a a footstep on the street, not a living soul around
to tip my barrel on its cart and help me home.

I sat shivering with cold and in despair—
till someone started toward me.
I saw his lanky hair—his feet were bare,
he wore a threadbare cloak—
which made me sure he was "The Hermit"
(our eccentric Francis Abbott)
—yet there was something unfamiliar to his face.
"I'll help you with your barrel," he said,
tipping it onto the handcart, and pushing it up Front Street
—where he stopped at an alley, and pointed down it, saying,
"It's late now, why not leave it here with my things?
Can you see them—those beams down there?
Don't worry, no one will take it. Nobody's interested, really.

"I know what you're thinking," he continued,
"that without your prop you'll lose your message.
But I promise you, you don't need it anymore.
It's like an old body—more of a bother than anything.
But you've gotten so used to it,
you can't imagine you could ever do without it.
But, look—if anybody takes it—
or tries to scrape it off in splinters
—(to sell for souvenirs—the way they've done with mine),

I could make you another: my father was a carpenter.
Now I see I've frightened you—
you're not sure what to make of me.
And you're right: there are lots of crazy people out there.


"Sometimes when I walk along these streets,
I'll look into the windows—
and see a workman sleeping, with a weary arm across his wife
—or the two of them, watching sleepless through the night
at the sickbed of their child
—or moving together through the unfathomable motions
of their sweet tender animal passions
—in the dance that makes their cells combine.
And through it all—always on the wall above their heads—
they've got that prop—
that dying image with its arms outstretched.
But it was *life*—
not *death*—I wanted them to think about.


"But they never get it right, do they?—
they can't believe that what actually might *save* them
might actually lie inside them.
And so they keep petitioning someone (who they
believe is a zillion light-years off in space—
and presumably busy, keeping the whole thing spinning)
to stop and explain it—or at least take away some of the misery.
I thought that maybe here with all this roaring,
I wouldn't hear them for a moment.
Yet I think that if they stopped—if they finally got it right—
I would honestly miss them—
and that touching, ridiculous condition:
their *humanness*."

"Come," he said, and he was hurrying ahead
—not turning—*even once*—to
see—if I were able to keep up—or even following.
And though I didn't marvel at it then,
I moved as easily as if I had been twenty.
And I could see him so clearly
that I wondered, for an instant, whether I had made him up.
But when we stopped on the Honeymoon Bridge,
and he laid his broad hand on my shoulder,
every doubt in me dissolved, every cell began to pulse.
Eternity came and went—And the Bridal Veil
kept pounding on its boulders
—And the Horseshoe kept pouring
from the green arc of its crest.


"Think of it," he said, "In the minute that we've watched,
*thirteen million tons* have fallen from that edge.
If you try to add it up—drop upon drop—year upon year,
you'll begin to comprehend 'eternity.'
And you'll start to wonder how a single drop
could remain in its source
—*when so much has kept pouring*
*through the lifetimes of a thousand generations!*
And then you'll start to believe it will never stop
—or never even change.
But look here," he touched my shoulder
and turned me to the north.
"Can you see those lights in the distance?—
that's Lewiston—where the Falls were born.


"Try to picture their beginning—when the glaciers started thawing,
and, south of here (near what you know as Buffalo),

the new Lake Erie began to melt—
and sent a jet of water overflowing to the north
—and the Niagara River began to run.
Its course crossed a wide plateau,
which dropped down a steep escarpment,
but—*just like you*—it went ahead and plunged
—and the Niagara Falls were born.
In time," he gently squeezed my arm,
"the limestone at their base began to crumble
—as *ten trillion tons of water* fell and pooled against it.
And the rocks above it fissured and crashed down
—and the Niagara Gorge was formed.

"As the river raced northward, the gorge eroded in its wake—
gouging out a channel through the steep plateau
—and the Falls moved south.
Sometimes a single inch took several centuries
—sometimes several yards went all at once—
till the Falls have moved ten miles from the place of their beginning
to where we're standing now."
"From Lewiston?" I asked (to show him I'd been listening).
"Yes," he took my hand,
"But that first hour, there was no one here
to note when they began—
or how magnificent they were—
when only the forest, sky—and I—stood above them.
—Did you know that someday *they'll be gone?*"

"Gone?" I asked, letting go his hand.
"Yes," he replied, "There'll only be the gorge
—channeled all the way to Buffalo
—with a shallow river running in its trough.

But nothing to plunge over—*no Niagara Falls!*—
nothing remarkable at all.
But that will take a billion years, and there'll be no one here
to remark the loss (except myself of course).
There'll be no forest then—(and not much of a sky).
I could show you where they were when I was born and when I died.
I've watched them all my life
—every year or so, I'll see some dog survive—
Crawl out. And shake its coat.
But you, Annie Taylor, *you* were different—

"you were capable of thought. You didn't
come by chance—you came to *save* your life!
—and you relied on your own wits
(though you'd heard the learned scientists
insist no one could do it).
You were threatened by police and politicians.
But despite them all (and your natural mortal dread),
you went ahead—you met your *destiny!*
—Of course, your whole idea was crazy.
Yet I thrilled to see you go. And who am I to criticize?—
You've seen me hanging with my arms outstretched—
not looking my best—or worthy of anyone's confidence.
But then, the essence of both our schemes
is in the part that *can't* be seen."

[ E PLURIBUS ]

"I had always *known* someone would make it,"
he turned to look at me,
"but I'd seen so many others—
the accidents and suicides—
I began to wonder when you'd come.

And it warmed my heart to *see* just who you were
—not some scientist or athlete—but that tiny teacher,
I'd seen so many times—in that outlandish feathered hat!
—I even heard you lie about your age!
You made me feel so pleased with the human race.
Despite all the predictable ones,
the ones who spend their lifetimes, humming the old hymns,
I always find a few with some surprises.

"In the years ahead, others will follow you,
but none of them remotely like yourself
—or even Bobby Leach—
that little song-and-dance man, who riles you so.
(Let me confide—though I'll be sorry to see him go—
he'll die of gangrene, next year in New Zealand
after slipping on an orange rind.)
But there'll be half a dozen others—(all men)—
dropping over in rubberized balls,
so safely enclosed they won't even know
when their journey begins or ends.
And not one of them will have dared to set a toe
on the Niagara—if you hadn't proved it could be done.

"For now, the Niagara is illimitable—
it takes no note of human scale.
But in time, more men (the busy, grasping kind)
will devise their ways to tinker with it.
They'll strip away its grandeur—
they'll harness it and humble it—
as if they had *created* it!
It would break your heart to see" (he took my hand and held it),
"how later in this century, they'll siphon half that splendor—
to drive the engines of their power mills.

—Oh, they'll leave some for the tourists—
but those emerald tones that gleam from the depth of its volume
*will be gone.*

"And yet," he dropped my hand and laughed,
"there still will be enough to keep them all amazed!
At night they'll project their tawdry, colored lights
onto its pure, shining brilliance,
and everyone will say it's an improvement—
as they gaze upon its tutti-frutti shades
and watch its plume of spray
rise up like cotton candy!
One day the Army engineers will shut the whole thing off
—so they can anchor down the rocks that have piled at its base,
and they'll leave the eager honeymooners
(who've been journeying here for days)
—to stand appalled before a naked promontory.

"Later, by Hyde Park, the corrosive things they'll dump
will burn the feet of children as they play among the weeds.
And over near Bill Love's canal, while families lie asleep,
the fumes from what they'll bury
will seep into their rooms.
And all along the river
—where barrels will lie rusting underground—
their poisons will leech out—
channeling a course—straight for the gorge—
that will make the Niagara
the greatest source of . . ."
He turned from the gorge and looked at me,
"But you don't know what I mean—and it's better that you don't.

"Yet I can't stop marveling at their knack for destroying things
—(much more quickly than anyone can make them).

But nothing *I* have said has ever stopped them.
You know as well as I *(I've heard you tell them)*
that nothing's going to change
—until a *change* begins *inside* them.
For now, all you should know
is that—till there's no one left to see it—
Niagara will remain a source of wonder
—that tells about the awesome, fragile beauty of the world
—And though no one will even know your name,
you'll remain, *Annie Taylor,*
Niagara's awesome and fragile *queen.*"

[ SIC TRANSIT ]

"But come," he said, pulling my hand,
"I want to show you something else—
I mustn't leave you the impression you'll be totally forgotten.
In fact there'll be a niche for you
—maybe *not* what you'd have planned—
but I can tell you, firsthand,
that their 'images' aren't meant to *represent* us.
—No, they make them to give comfort to themselves
—by projecting their hopes or fears onto someone else—
Or to help them contemplate 'the great ideas'
—that they feel too small to think of on their own."

Then he rushed ahead of me—
as swift as a sudden wind, gusting west across the bridge span—
and no matter how I tried,
I couldn't match his pace.
And as the space between us grew,
I moved more slowly—
I limped—and (when I fell) I thought of giving up.
And when he slipped completely from my sight,

my eyes fell back into their tunnel
—and I was sure that I'd be lost out there *forever* in the dark
—And I wondered if he'd *ever* been there at all.


I told my feet to take me *back*—but something forced me forward—
to cross the bridge and find where he had gone.
And so, I stumbled on—till a ramp descended,
and a thousand lights broke out above me,
and I recognized Clifton Hill—
rising above the shore—where (twenty years before),
I'd landed in my barrel at its dock.
But now I found no throngs of cheering people,
no steeples with pealing bells—
only rows of darkened stores—with gaudy colored signs
that winked above their windows and their doors.


I entered one, where I recognized Queen Victoria
(standing regally in her mourning dress and veil)
beside the natty (but uncouth) Werewolf of London
(with his hirsute face and unmanicured nails)
—the pair of them waxen and lifesize.
Through another door I entered a museum,
devoted entirely to my contemporary:
Harry Houdini
—"the first human being," a sign proclaimed,
"to escape from a regulation straitjacket,
used by the murderous insane."


The room beyond was rounded—*Like a barrel!*—
and as I entered, it began to spin.
And as I struggled to get through, it spun more quicky
—till I fell to my hands and knees and began to crawl.
I spotted then below me, a drop of something red

*—just as the floor whirled up to be the ceiling!*
And when it whirled back down,
the bloody drop was *gone*.
And oh, I wanted to *believe* in him
—to believe I wasn't there alone—that *he* was with me—
and would let me close my eyes and lead me through.

The place I staggered to was dark (with several rows of seats).
And as I sat to catch my breath,
the seat began to move
and rushed me through the rapids—to the brink of the precipice—
and over *the Falls!*
—where I'd gone before—but much more willingly.
When it finally stopped, I stepped into a corridor
—and turning a corner, passed a heap of plaster rocks
—and saw a barrel!—*my original barrel!*—
with *"Queen of the Mist"* still scrawled across its staves
(I ran from it—as if I'd seen my lover in the grave).

I found myself in a room
where, though the lights were dim—
I could see a woman: she was blond and slim
in a white lace blouse
—standing absolutely still as I approached
—Even as I called to her (so she wouldn't be afraid)
—Even as I drew so close—that I could see
the spurt of blood that was trickling down her brow
and the dazed look on her face
(which made me think she'd understand
what I'd been through).

She seemed too stunned to speak
(I guessed I'd given her a fright—when she thought she was alone).

Yet for a moment, I still hoped that she would greet me—
that she'd raise her hand to wave. Or comfort me.
But then I glanced below her waist—
and saw a *thing* that was meant to be *a barrel!*
It was painted red with carnival designs!
I had to turn my eyes to spare myself
more pain—but as I did—I
glimpsed—the sign above her head,
and read *my name.*


[ LAST DAYS ]

My last few years, on dry weather days,
I'd sit outside the International Hotel on Falls Street.
I could barely see at all—just a glimpse now and then—
as if through a keyhole.
But I had a cane
and knew my way by touch.
I'd bring the pillow from my bed
and set it on the steps,
so I could sit (close to the railing)
—and spread a handful of my postcards
beside my metal cup.

If the traffic got too heavy,
or there were complaints—
or some function for the gentry
—they'd send the bellhop out—to make me move.
Then I'd take my pillow to the curb—
along with the hatbox
that I used
for carrying the cards and cup—
and set it up as a table

to display the few things I had left
—on the same level with the passing horses' hooves.

Sometimes a hackman would point me out.
And then a gentleman or lady
—(I couldn't tell until I heard the voice)—
might pass a coin to the driver for a card.
Sometimes, with a bit of prompting,
a child's voice might call hello.
And occasionally, someone leaned in my direction
and posed a serious question
—but before I could frame a serious reply,
the reins would snap,
and the voices roll away.

Sometimes someone passing
would drop a nickel in my cup
—thinking me a beggar—or at best an old peddler
with some faded cards to sell
—not imagining I had anything to tell—
seeing me crumpled on that curb, so spattered and so small.
Yet inside I still felt vast as the Niagara—
though we both were tired now
and didn't bother to get riled
when they ignored us or abused us
or took us for something else.

I had lost my barrel in an alley one night
—when strange wild winds
came ripping through the Falls
and blew apart my booth.
Perhaps my banner struck me
(at least that's what they told me

when I started to describe what I had seen).
I never found my barrel after that
—Though at first, I searched for it daily.
But in the end, all the alleys looked alike.
And all the barrels were filled with rain.

I've wondered—was it true—as someone told me—
that I didn't need a prop to tell my story.
But I never put his theory to the test.
After that, I kept my history to myself
—as well as that message
that I'd dragged from place to place
for twenty years—at such expense:
I used to tell them, *I am alive*—
I had thought that was a gift,
but now it seems too thin and tattered
to be of use to anyone.

I can't explain, but now and then,
I sometimes see his face
—not a resurrected face as in our dreams—
but something present and yet distant—
Like mist. Or time. Or space.
At first, I thought he was "The Hermit"—
with his strangeness—And those visions
and those prophecies.
Though now I think he was something else.
—But *who* would come to hold my hand—
then leave me here to find the answers for myself?

I guess they'll tell you
how they brought me to the poorhouse
—as if they should be praised.

And they'll say I came "to nothing"
—as if I ought to be ashamed.
And they'll mention I was sick
and eighty-three and blind
—and "should have known better"—
when I sat out on a curb, selling postcards in the sun
to keep myself alive.
But I ask you: *What else could I have done?*

# Acknowledgments

I wish to express my grateful acknowledgment to *Ontario Review,* where the first section of *Queen of the Mist* was originally published.

I also wish to express my gratitude to the following organizations: the Niagara Council on the Arts for so much indispensable assistance; the New York State Council on the Arts for the Writer in Residence grants that first brought me to Niagara; the National Endowment for the Arts for the Poetry Fellowship that supported the beginning of this book; and to Yaddo and the MacDowell Colony for the residencies during which I wrote and revised it. Special thanks to the Niagara Falls Public Library's Local History Division for their invaluable research assistance and for permission to use the images of Annie Taylor.

My gratitude also extends to several individuals who offered assistance and encouragement during various stages of this undertaking: Hayden Carruth, Joyce Carol Oates, Raymond Smith, Richard Howard, Jonathan Galassi, Marge Piercy, Colette Inez, Jacquie Lodico, and especially Amy Caldwell.

*Queen of the Mist* was the runner-up for the Poetry Society of America's Alice Fay di Castagnola Award.